THE

Cookbook

FOR **Easy Bake Oven**

with **ACTIVITY Pages**

Adult Supervision Required

Printed in the United States of America

ISBN 978-1-7371396-2-1

Desserts MENU
Table of Contents

Important Please Read

Note to our newest Jr Chef:

Welcome to the Hasty Tasty Family! We can't wait to see what you create! You can use your new cookbook to make your very own individual sized cakes, cookies, and more in just a matter of minutes. Don't forget to take pictures because we would love to see what you have made!

Ready to get started? The very first thing you will need to do is pick out the lucky person that gets to be your adult assistant and helps you all along the way! All great chefs have one! Hmmm…who will it be?

What bakery is complete without a menu? **Take a look at your bakery signs beginning on page 37.** You have your very own menu, order page, open & closed signs and more!

Note to Adult assistant (Adult assistance /supervision required.)

I would **HIGHLY** encourage you to read the tips below to make your experience the best it can be. The Egg suggestion is a game changer.

As a super fun activity, we have included bakery signs, a menu, an order form, and more! The menu coincides with the cookbook! Take a look at page 37!

Also, check out our Youtube® channel and facebook® page (Hasty Tasty Chef) for fun bakery activities and great videos. Watch your little chef discover the magical fun of turning their toy bake oven into a mini-bakery in minutes!

Helpful Tips for Ingredients

All of the recipes are individual sized, therefore, the ingredients needed will be in small amounts. For example, the recipe may call for 1 tbsp of dry pudding mix rather than the entire box. In order to keep your pantry stocked for your little baker and to not be wasteful, we have found the following tricks work well!

Eggs: If a recipe calls for eggs, it's normally only a tbsp. This is less than 1 egg. **I like to keep something like egg beaters® on hand to use.** It makes it very simple and convenient. If I don't have it, I will whisk an egg and then measure out 1 tbsp.

Dry Mixes (example pudding or gelatin mix such as Jello ®): I empty mine into a small airtight container and label. I use what is needed and save the rest for the next recipe!

Once you test out this book, would you please consider leaving a review on Amazon? It really helps out others like yourself that may be wondering if this book is also right for them. I **really** would appreciate it so much!

I sincerely hope that your little one enjoys this book as much as I did writing it for them

Choc & Peanut Butter
Page 8

Chocolate Cake
Page 8

Vanilla Cake
Page 9

Banana Split
Page 10

CAKES

Peanut Butter & Chocolate
Page 11

Peanut Butter & Jelly
Page 11

Red Velvet
Page 12

Unicorn Cake
Page 13

Choc Covered Strawberry
Page 14

Cookies & Cream
Page 15

Cake Mix Brownies
Page 16

Base Mix from Scratch

Let's Get Ready!

- 2 ¼ cup all-purpose flour

- 1 ¼ cup Sugar

- 1 tablespoon baking powder

- ½ teaspoon salt

- 12 baggies (ex. Ziploc®) Snack size works great

1 Measure all dry ingredients and mix together VERY well by sifting together into a bowl.

2 Sift all ingredients together into a second bowl to make sure well mixed. I normally do this a couple of times back and forth between the two bowls.

3 Divide the combined mix into 12 equal portions and place into the sandwich or snack size baggies (about 4 tablespoons mix into each baggie).

4 Print out the Hasty Tasty Coloring Toppers (see next page) and turn boring bags into your very own personalized bakery mixes!

Base Mix from Box

Use any flavor of boxed cake mix to make these simple ready made cake mix packs for individual sized Cakes! Chocolate, Yellow, & Strawberry flavors are always good!

Recipe for Box Mix Cakes or cupcakes, using this Base Mix Recipe, is found on bottom of page 9

Let's Get Ready!

- 1 Box Store Bought Cake Mix (any flavor)

- 15 baggies (ex. Ziploc ®)

Let's Do It!

1 Divide the cake mix into equal portions of 4 tablespoons each and place each portion in sandwich or snack size baggies.

2 Print out the Hasty Tasty Coloring Toppers (see next page) and label back with cake mix flavor. Easily turn boring bags into your very own personalized bakery mixes!

FREE Personalized Package Toppers

Time to get your base mixes ready! It's easy, quick and makes it so simple when you get ready to cook your individual cakes! You can choose to make packs of cake base mix from scratch, from box mix, or from BOTH! In just a couple of minutes, you will have **12-15 packs** (depending on scratch or box recipe) of cake mix ready to go! Its SO easy and saves you so much time!

Adult helpers: Check out our **video** on the Hasty Tasty Chef Youtube channel and follow along with us while we make our base mix packs! BONUS: Grab a FREE printable topper set to color! This will turn boring bags of mix into a FUN activity while creating your very own personalized bakery mixes!!

Step 1:   Visit   **www.FreeTopper.com**

       Choose from Set A (*Unicorns, Mermaids, etc...*)

       Or Set B (*Pirates, Sharks, etc...*)

Set A   **Set B**

Step 2:   Print & Cut along dotted lines.

Step 3:   Color your topper. Get creative & have fun!

Step 4:   Fold your topper in half. Place each one over the top of your individually bagged mixes and staple on the top.

Follow along with us on our Hasty Tasty Chef Youtube channel and we can make our base mix recipe and toppers together!

★ CHOCOLATE CAKE

From Scratch

Makes 1 small cake or 6 cupcakes

Let's Get Ready!

- 1 Pack **Scratch** Mix (from page 6)

- 3 tablespoons milk

- 1 ½ tablespoons dry unsweetened cocoa powder

- 1 tablespoons melted unsalted butter

- 1 tablespoon beaten egg

- ½ tablespoon Chocolate Instant pudding mix (dry)

- 1 teaspoon sugar

Let's Cook!

1. Preheat oven according to manufacturers directions. Typically around 20 minutes.

2. Warm milk in microwave for 8 seconds. Set aside. Slightly melt butter (about 10-15 seconds).

3. Mix together dry cocoa powder and melted butter. Add in dry chocolate pudding mix.

4. Stir in milk and egg. Mix well.

5. Add in sugar and 1 individual pack of scratch base mix from page 6. Mix until moistened.

6. Spray pan with nonstick spray. Pour batter into pan and cook for about 17-19 minutes. Carefully remove and cool. Top with frosting of choice.

CHOCOLATE & PEANUT BUTTER

Let's Get Ready!

Cake: See Cake Recipe Above

- 3 tablespoons powdered sugar

- 1 tablespoon butter

- 3 tablespoons peanut butter

- 1 tablespoon milk

Let's Cook!

1. Cook chocolate cake. Use recipe above for scratch or box mix recipe on page 9 using chocolate mix.

2. Peanut Butter Frosting: In a small bowl mix milk, butter and peanut butter.

3. Slowly add in powdered sugar and mix well.

4. Top chocolate cake with peanut butter frosting

Vanilla Cake
From Scratch

Makes 1 small cake or 6 cupcakes

Let's Get Ready!

- 1 Pack Base Mix (from page 6) Scratch

- 1 tbsp slightly melted unsalted butter

- 2 tablespoons Milk

- 1 tablespoon beaten egg

- ¼ teaspoon vanilla (optional)

Let's Cook!

1. Preheat oven according to manufactures instructions. Typically around 20 minutes

2. Slightly melt the butter in the microwave (about 10-15 seconds).

3. Combine melted butter, milk, vanilla, and cake base mix pack. Stir just until slightly moistened .

4. Add egg and stir just until mixed well.

5. Spray pan with nonstick spray and pour batter into prepared pan. Cook for approximately 16-18 minutes or until done.

6. Carefully remove, cool, and top with frosting of choice

 # Cake or Cupcakes From Box Mix

Let's Get Ready!

- 1 Pack of **Box** Cake Base mix (from page 6)

- 1 tablespoon slightly melted butter

- 2 tablespoons Milk

- 1 tablespoon beaten egg

Let's Cook!

1. Preheat oven according to manufactures instructions. Typically around 20 minutes

2. Slightly melt the butter in the microwave (about 10-15 seconds).

3. Combine melted butter, milk, vanilla, and cake base mix pack. Stir just until slightly moistened .

4. Add egg and stir just until mixed well.

5. Spray pan with nonstick spray and pour batter into prepared pan. Cook for approximately 16-18 minutes or until done.

6. Carefully remove, cool, and top with frosting of choice

BANANA SPLIT CAKE

Let's Get Ready!

Cake

- See page 9 for cake ingredients. Can use scratch or box mix recipe.

Topping

- 2 tablespoons dry instant vanilla pudding mix
- ½ cup Milk
- 2 tablespoons crushed pineapple (drained)
- ½ banana (sliced)
- 4-5 Strawberries (sliced)
- ½ cup whipped topping (ex. Coolwhip®)
- Chocolate syrup to drizzle

Let's Cook!

1. Follow the recipe on page 9 to cook the vanilla cake. You can use scratch or box mix recipe. I like to cook two cakes and stack them together to make one thick cake, but that's optional.

2. In a small bowl, whisk pudding mix with milk. Whisk until it thickens.

3. Poke about 6-8 holes in the top of the cake all the way through. I used a chopstick to do this, but you can use anything similar in size.

4. Spread ½ of the prepared pudding mixture over the cake.

5. Add a layer of crushed pineapple to top.

6. Add a layer of sliced strawberries.

7. Spread remaining pudding mixture on top.

8. Add a layer of sliced bananas.

9. Add whipped topping on top and drizzle with chocolate syrup.

This is one of my favorites!! Even though there's a few steps, it's super EASY to make! You won't regret it!

PEANUT BUTTER & CHOCOLATE

Makes 1 small cake or 6 cupcakes

From Scratch

Let's Get Ready!

Cake

- 1 Pack Scratch Base Mix (from page 6)
- 1 ½ tablespoons Milk
- 1 ½ tablespoons Peanut Butter
- 1 tablespoon melted butter
- 1 tablespoon egg
- Chocolate frosting

Let's Cook!

1. Preheat oven according to manufacturers directions. Spray pan with nonstick cooking spray

2. In a small bowl, mix together milk, peanut butter, melted butter and egg. Mix until well blended. Slowly whisk in pack of scratch cake mix.

3. Pour batter into prepared pan. Only fill pan ¾ full.

4. Cook the cake for approximately 18-20 minutes

5. Carefully remove and cool.

6. Top with chocolate frosting. Recipe can be found on page 34 or you may use store bought.

PEANUT BUTTER & JELLY

Let's Get Ready!

Cake: See Cake Recipe Above

- 3 tablespoons jelly of choice
- 3 tablespoons powdered sugar
- 1 tablespoon butter
- 3 tablespoons peanut butter
- 1 tablespoon milk

Let's Cook!

1. Follow the recipe above to cook Peanut Butter cake. Do not use the chocolate frosting in step 6 above when making this recipe. Cut cake in half to make 2 layers and set aside.

2. Frosting: Mix milk, butter and peanut butter. Slowly add in powdered sugar and mix well.

3. Spread layer of Jelly over cake (about 11/2 tbsp). Top with ½ of the peanut butter mixture from step 2.

4. Add the second layer of peanut butter cake and repeat step 3.

Red Velvet Cake

From Box Mix

Makes 1 small cake or 6 cupcakes

Let's Get Ready!

- 1 pack of Red Velvet Box Base mix from page 6

- 2 tablespoons Milk

- 1 tablespoon slightly melted butter

- 1 tablespoon beaten egg

Let's Cook!

1 Preheat oven according to manufacturers directions. Spray pan with nonstick cooking spray.

2 Whisk together milk, butter, & egg. Slowly add in pack of red velvet cake base. Mix well.

3 Pour cake batter into prepared pan.

4 Cook for approximately 16 minutes. Carefully remove and cool.

5 Top with cream cheese frosting. Recipe found on page 34 or you may use store bought.

Make Your Very Own Magical Bakery!

Use the cutouts beginning on page 36 to create a fun magical bakery. Signs, name tags, play money & more! You'll even have a bakery menu that goes hand in hand with your cookbook! Use it to take your orders and then serve up your very own fresh baked cake or cookie!

UNICORN CAKE

Let's Cook!

Cake

- 4 Packs of Base Mix (scratch or box pg 6)
- ½ cup milk
- 4 tablespoons slightly melted unsalted butter
- 1 egg beaten
- 4 different food coloring of choice

Frosting

- 6 tablespoons Whipped Topping (ex. Coolwhip®)
- 1 tablespoon Instant Vanilla Pudding mix
- 1 tablespoon Milk

1 Preheat oven according to manufacturers directions. Spray pan with nonstick cooking spray.

2 In a small bowl, mix room temperature milk and melted butter together. Slowly whisk in the 4 packs of cake mix base. Add in beaten egg. Mix until moistened.

3 Divide batter equally into 4 separate bowls. Add a few drops of different food color to each bowl to get your 4 different color cakes. Mix well.

4 Pour batter from one bowl into prepared pan and cook for approximately 16-18 minutes or until done. Carefully remove cake and cool.

5 Repeat step 4 for remaining 3 colors.

Frosting

6 Combine all ingredients together for frosting in a small bowl. Whisk very well until thickened.

7 Place 1st layer of cake on serving plate. Top with a small amount of frosting to hold cakes together. Repeat for layers 2 and 3. Add the last layer of cake to top and then spread remaining frosting on top. Tip: Add sprinkles or a little colored sugar to top for an extra "pop" of color! You can also cut into six servings as pictured on page 5 for bite sized cake

If a holiday is near, make your "Special Cake of the Day" a holiday colored cake using the recipe above. For example, you could make a red & green cake around Christmas, a red/ pink cake around Valentine's Day and a green cake around Saint Patrick's Day!

Chocolate Covered Strawberry

Let's Cook!

Cake

- 1 pack of Strawberry base mix from Box (page 6)
- 2 tablespoons Milk
- 1 tablespoon slightly melted Butter
- 1 tablespoon beaten egg

Topping

- 6 tablespoons Whipped Topping (example Coolwhip®)
- 1 tablespoon Instant Chocolate Pudding mix
- 1 tablespoon Milk
- ¼ cup fresh sliced Strawberries

1 Preheat oven according to manufacturer directions. Spray pan with nonstick cooking spray.

2 In a small bowl, stir together room temperature milk, and egg. Slowly add in cake mix and melted butter. Mix until combined.

3 Pour batter into prepared pan and cook for approximately 15-17 minutes. Carefully remove and cool

4 Combine all topping ingredients (except for strawberries) together in a small bowl. Whisk very well until thickened. Apply to top of cake.

5 Layer sliced strawberries over whipped topping.

If you prefer Strawberries & Cream instead of chocolate, use vanilla pudding mix in place of the chocolate pudding mix when you make the frosting.

Cookies & Cream

Makes 1 small cake or 6 cupcakes   **From Scratch or Box**

Let's Get Ready!

Chocolate cake

- See recipe on pg. 8 or 9 (scratch or box)

Cream Topping

- 1 ounce softened cream cheese

- 3 tablespoons softened butter

- 1 tablespoon Milk

- ¾ cup powdered sugar

- 4 Chocolate Cookies (example Oreo ®) crushed well (I put them in a baggie to crush up)

Lets Cook!

1 Cook Chocolate cake following recipe You can use the scratch cake recipe on page 8 or box mix recipe on page 9. Cook 2 cakes to make a layered cake. (If you only want one layer, cut topping ingredients in half). Set cake aside.

2 Cream together cream cheese and butter. Add milk and mix well.

3 Slowly add in powdered sugar and mix well.

4 Add in finely crushed cookies and mix well.

5 Spread Cookies and Cream frosting on top of chocolate cake and enjoy!

Make YOUR OWN Magic

Cake Mix Brownies

Let's Get Ready!

- 1 Pack Chocolate Base Mix from BOX (page 6)

- ½ tablespoon melted butter

- ½ tablespoon milk

- ½ tablespoon beaten egg (I like to use something like egg beaters ®)

- 1 ½ tablespoons semisweet chocolate chips

Let's Cook!

1 Preheat oven according to manufacturers directions. Usually around 20 minutes. Spray pan with nonstick cooking spray.

2 Slightly melt butter (about 10-12 seconds). Stir in milk and base mix pack.

3 Stir in egg and chocolate chips. Mix very well. Mixture will be very thick.

4 Spread batter into prepared pan. The batter will only cover about 2/3 of the pan. Cook for approximately 16-18 minutes. Brownie may not appear to be done, but it will continue to set up as it cools. Carefully remove and cool.

Eat these brownies alone or use to serve up a brownie ice cream sundae! Brownie, vanilla ice cream, whipped topping, chocolate syrup & sprinkles. Mmmmmm…..

Cookies

Menu of the Day

Strawberries & Cream
Pg. 19

Lemonade Cookies
Pg. 20

Chocolate Pudding Cookie
Pg. 21

Cooking TIP: *Most of the cookie recipes make 6-8 cookies. Rather than crowding them all on one pan, you can choose to cook 4 at a time.*

Snickerdoodle Cookies
Pg. 22

Chocolate Chip Cookies
Pg. 23

Sprinkles Cookies
Pg. 24

Makes 8 Bags of Mix!

Let's Get Ready!

- 2 cups all-purpose flour
- 2 ½ tablespoons white sugar
- 1 teaspoon baking soda
- ¼ teaspoon salt
- 8 snack or sandwich sized Baggies

Let's Cook!

1 Combine all ingredients together in a medium bowl. Stir together very well.

2 Sift the ingredients together into a second bowl. I do this a couple of times, back and forth between the two bowls, to make sure it is very well mixed.

3 Divide the mix up evenly by placing 5 tablespoons of well mixed base mix into each of the 8 snack or sandwich sized baggies. You may have a small amount left over. Just divide the extra up between the 8 baggies so that they are all even.

4 Print out the Coloring Toppers (see page 7 for instructions) and turn boring bags into your very own personalized bakery mixes!

5 Color your toppers and label the back "Cookie Base Mix". Add your packages of Hasty Tasty Cookie Mix into your bakery pantry.

Bake Someone Happy Today!

Strawberries & Cream Cookies

Let's Cook!

Let's Get Ready!

- 1 pack of cookie base mix (page 18)

- 1 ½ tablespoons of dry strawberry gelatin mix (ex. Jello ®)

- 2 teaspoons plain yogurt

- 1 tablespoon melted unsalted butter

- 1 ½ tablespoons of white chocolate chips

1. Preheat oven according to manufacturers directions. Spray pan with nonstick cooking spray. Melt butter (about 15 seconds) and set aside.

2. In a small bowl, mix together one package of cookie base mix and dry strawberry gelatin mix.

3. Add melted butter to dry mixture from step 2 and mix well. Next, add in egg and mix together. Will form a "dough"

4. Divide dough into 6 portions. Roll each one in hands to form a small ball and then flatten slightly. Place in pan.

5. Sprinkle white chocolate chips on top and push down slightly.

6. Cook for approximately 12 minutes. Carefully remove & let cool. Cookies will be soft, but will firm up as they cool.

Do you like Chocolate Covered Strawberries better than Strawberries & Cream? Here's an idea: Substitute semi-sweet chocolate chips or milk chocolate chips instead of white chocolate chips! Delicious!

Let's Cook!

Let's Get Ready!

- 1 pack of cookie base mix (page 18)

- 1 ½ tablespoons of dry Lemon gelatin mix (ex. Jello ®)

- 1 tablespoon beaten egg

- 1 tablespoon melted unsalted butter

- 2 tablespoons powdered sugar to roll cookies in

1 Preheat oven according to manufacturers directions. Spray pan with nonstick cooking spray. Melt butter 10-15 seconds) and set aside.

2 In a small bowl, mix together one package of cookie base mix and dry lemon gelatin mix.

3 Add melted butter to dry mixture from step 2. Mix well. Next, add in egg. Mix well to form a "dough"

4 Divide into 6 portions. Roll each one in hands to form a "ball" and then flatten slightly so that it will fit into pan without being too high. Can cook 4 at a time if you want.

5 Cook for approximately 11-13 minutes. Carefully remove.

6 Roll "cookie" in powdered sugar to coat well. Cookie will be soft when warm, but will harden as it cools.

LEMONADE

Bakery **Idea**

Here's a "Special" twist: Make "Lemon Sandwich Cookies" by putting two cookies together with a little Cream Cheese Frosting (page 34) in the center!

Chocolate Pudding Cookies

Let's Get Ready!

- 1 pack of cookie base mix (page 18)

- 1 ½ tablespoons dry chocolate pudding mix

- 1 tablespoon beaten egg

- 1 ½ tablespoons melted unsalted butter

- 1 tablespoons chocolate chips

Let's Cook!

1. Preheat oven according to manufactures directions. Spray pan with nonstick cooking spray. Melt butter (10-15seconds) and set aside.

2. In a small bowl, mix together pack of cookie base and dry pudding mix.

3. Add melted butter to dry mixture from step 2. Mix well. Next, add egg and mix to form a "dough"

4. Divide into 6 portions. Roll each one in hands and then flatten slightly to fit into pan without being too tall.

5. Sprinkle chocolate chips on top and push down into cookie slightly.

6. Cook for approximately 11-13. Carefully remove & let cool. Cookies will be very soft when you first remove. They will firm up as they cool.

Makes 6 cookies

Want to make a Chocolate-Peanut Butter cookie? Sprinkle peanut butter chips on top of the cookie (step #5) instead of chocolate chips!

Snickerdoodle Cookies

Let's Get Ready!

- 1 pack of cookie base mix (page 18)

- 1 tablespoon brown sugar

- 1 tablespoon white granulated sugar

- 1 tablespoon whisked egg

- 1 tablespoon melted unsalted butter

Topping

- 1 teaspoon granulated sugar

- ¼ teaspoon cinnamon

Let's Cook!

1 Preheat oven according to manufacturers directions. Spray pan with nonstick cooking spray. Melt butter (about 10-15 seconds) and set aside.

2 In a separate small bowl, combine one package of cookie base mix, brown sugar, and white sugar. Mix very well.

3 Add in egg to the dry mixture from step 2 and stir slightly. Add in melted butter. Mix well. Will form a cookie "dough"

4 Divide dough into 6-8 parts. Roll each part in your hands to form a "ball". Flatten slightly to fit into pan without being too tall. Can cook 4 at a time if you want

5 Combine topping ingredients together and then sprinkle on top of cookies. Press topping into cookie. You may have extra left over (depends on how sweet you want the cookie).

6 Cook for approximately 11-13 minutes. Carefully remove & let cool. Cookies will be very soft when they are warm, but they will firm up as they cool.

Baked Fresh Daily

Chocolate Chip Cookies

MAKES 6-8 COOKIES

Let's Get Ready!

- 1 single pack of cookie base mix (page 18)

- 2 tablespoons Brown sugar

- 1 tablespoon whisked egg

- 1 tablespoon melted unsalted butter

- 1 tablespoon chocolate chips

Let's Cook!

1 Preheat oven according to manufacturers directions. Spray pan with nonstick cooking spray. Melt butter (about 10-15 seconds) and set aside.

2 In a separate small bowl, combine one package of cookie base mix and brown sugar. Mix very well.

3 Add in egg to the dry mixture from step 2 and stir slightly. Add in melted butter. Mix well. Will form a cookie "dough"

4 Divide dough into 6-8 parts. Roll each part in your hands to form a "ball". Flatten slightly to fit into pan without being too tall. Can cook 4 at a time if you want

5 Sprinkle chocolate chips onto the top of the cookie dough and press into cookie slightly.

6 Cook for approximately 11-13 minutes. Carefully remove & let cool. The cookies will be soft when you first remove them, but they will firm up as they cool.

Sprinkles cookie

MAKES 6-8 COOKIES

Let's Get Ready!

- 1 single pack of cookie base mix (page 18)

- 1 tablespoon Brown sugar

- 1 tablespoon granulated white sugar

- 1 tablespoon whisked egg

- 1 tablespoon melted unsalted butter

- 1 teaspoon sprinkles

Let's Cook!

1 Preheat oven according to manufacturers directions. Spray pan with nonstick cooking spray. Melt butter (about 10-15 seconds) and set aside.

2 In a separate small bowl, combine package of cookie base mix, brown sugar, and white sugar. Mix very well.

3 Add in egg to the dry mixture from step 2 and stir slightly. Add in melted butter. Mix well. Will form a cookie "dough"

4 Add in sprinkles. Save a few sprinkles to go on top of cookies.

5 Divide dough into 6-8 parts. Roll each part in your hands to form a "ball". Flatten slightly to fit into pan without being too tall. Add a few more sprinkles on top of cookies and press into cookie slightly. Can cook 4 cookies at a time if you choose.

6 Cook for approximately 11-13 minutes. Carefully remove and allow to cool. Cookies will be very soft while they are warm, but they will firm up as they cool.

Bakery Idea

Make a special cookie around the holidays! Change the sprinkle colors to match the holiday! You can do pastel for Easter or Red and Green for Christmas!

Too Good to Leave Out

Cinnamon Dessert Sticks
Page 26

Peanut Butter & Chocolate Pizza
Page 27

English Muffin Pizza
Page 28

Crescent Dough Pizza
Page 29

Strawberry Dessert Sticks
Page 30

Hot Ham & Cheese
Page 31

Cheese Breadsticks
Page 31

Chocolate Pancake
Page 31

Sprinkles Pancake
Page 32

CINNAMON
Dessert Pizza

Let's Get Ready!

- 2 pieces of crescent roll dough about ¾ the size of your pan
- 1 tablespoon melted butter
- 2 tablespoons brown sugar
- ½ teaspoon cinnamon

Glaze:

- 1 ½ tablespoons powdered sugar
- 1 teaspoon melted butter
- ½ teaspoon hot water

Let's Cook!

1. Preheat oven according to manufacturers directions. Spray pan with nonstick cooking spray.

2. In a small bowl, mix melted butter, brown sugar, and cinnamon together. Set aside.

3. Lay 1 piece of crescent roll dough in bottom of pan. Flatten to spread out. Top with ½ of the cinnamon mixture from step 2.

4. Add second layer of dough to top. Spread remaining cinnamon mixture from step 2 on top.

5. Cook for approximately 19-21 minutes. Remove and cool.

6. Combine all ingredients for glaze and drizzle over top of pizza. You can drizzle with a spoon or place glaze in the corner of a sandwich bag and snip a small piece of the corner off. I like to cut my "pizza" into strips to make Cinnamon sticks!

Love at First Bite

CHOCOLATE & PEANUT BUTTER Pizza

Let's Get Ready!

- 1 piece crescent roll dough about ¾ the size of your pan

- 1 tablespoon powdered sugar

- ½ tablespoon melted butter

- 1 ½ tablespoons peanut butter

- ½ tablespoon milk

- 2 tablespoons chocolate chips

Glaze

- 1 tablespoon melted butter

- 1 tablespoon peanut butter

- 1 ½ tablespoons powdered sugar

Let's Cook!

1. Preheat oven according to manufacturers directions. Spray pan with nonstick cooking spray.

2. Place crescent roll dough in pan. Spread out but leave just a little room around edge of pan

3. In a small bowl, combine powdered sugar, butter, and milk. Mix well. Spread on top of crescent dough.

4. Cook for 14-16 minutes. Remove.

5. Add chocolate chips to top and press in. They will start to melt in 2-3 minutes. Use the back of a spoon to gently run over the top of the chocolate chips to spread the melted chocolate out over the pizza.

To Make Glaze:

Mix melted butter and peanut butter together, Mix well. Slowly mix in powdered sugar.

Drizzle glaze over top of pizza. You can use a spoon or place glaze into a sandwich bag in one corner. To use sandwich bag: Snip the corner off and gently squeeze to drizzle over your pizza.

TOPPINGS

Bananas

Chocolate Drizzle

Caramel Drizzle

Candy

Nuts

Whipped Topping

Marshmallows

English Muffin Pizza

Let's Get Ready!

- 1 English Muffin

- 1 tablespoon olive oil (divided)

- 4 tablespoons pizza sauce (divided)

- 12-16 mini pepperoni (optional)

- Italian Herbs (basil, oregano mix)

- 4 tablespoons shredded cheese (divided)

Let's Cook!

1 Preheat oven according to manufacturers directions. Spray pan with nonstick spray

2 Please always ask your adult assistant to help: Slice the muffin horizontally into 4 thin slices. Each pizza will need to be cooked separately because of size. Slices will need to be flattened so they are not too tall after toppings are put on.

3 Brush olive oil on each one. Spread 1 tablespoon of pizza sauce on each one.

4 Place a dash of Italian herbs on each one. Sprinkle shredded cheese on top of each one of the pizzas.

5 Place 3-4 pepperoni on each pizza (optional)

6 Cook for approximately 9-11 minutes. Remove carefully and cool.

Best Pizza Ever
Delivery Available →

CRESCENT ROLL PIZZA

Let's Get Ready!

- 1 piece of crescent roll dough about ¾ the size of your pan

- ½ tablespoon melted butter

- 1/8 teaspoon garlic

- 1 tablespoon pizza sauce

- 1 tablespoon mozzarella cheese

- 6-8 mini pepperoni (optional)

- Italian herbs - Basil and oregano mix

Let's Cook!

1. Preheat oven according to manufacturers directions. Spray pan with nonstick spray

2. Spread dough out to cover the bottom of your pan.

3. Combine melted butter and garlic. Brush over your dough.

4. Spread the pizza sauce over the dough.

5. Sprinkle a dash of Italian herbs over the pizza sauce.

6. Sprinkle shredded cheese on pizza. Add pepperoni on top (optional).

7. Cook for approximately 11-13 minutes. Carefully remove and cool. Enjoy!

STRAWBERRY
Dessert Pizza

Let's Get Ready!

- 1 piece of crescent roll dough about ¾ the size of your pan

- 1 tablespoon strawberry jam

Glaze

- 1 tablespoon softened cream cheese

- 1 tablespoon softened butter

- 1 tablespoon powdered sugar

Let's Cook!

1. Preheat oven according to manufacturers directions. Spray pan with nonstick spray.

2. Place the piece of dough in your pan. Flatten out to cover the bottom.

3. Spread the strawberry jam over the uncooked dough.

4. Cook for approximately 11-13 minutes. Carefully remove.

5. To Make Glaze: Mix the softened cream cheese and butter together. If they are not softened, you can place in the microwave for about 8 seconds (cream cheese) 10 seconds for the butter.

6. Add in powdered sugar and mix well. This will form a glaze.

7. Drizzle glaze over your pizza using a spoon or use a sandwich bag by placing glaze in the corner of the bag and snipping corner off to drizzle out. I like to cut it in strips to make dessert sticks.

Abracadabra!

Hot Ham & Cheese

Let's Get Ready!

- 1 piece of crescent roll dough about the size of your pan

- Slice of ham

- Slice of Cheese

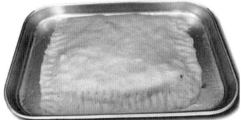

Let's Cook!

1 Preheat oven according to manufacturers directions. Spray pan with nonstick spray.

2 Place dough on pan. Place ham on ½ of the dough. Place cheese slice on top of ham. If ham slice too large, just cut down to size. ½ of the dough should be empty.

3 Fold empty side of dough over the top of cheese to form a "sandwich". Pinch the edges of the dough together to seal. I like to use a fork to press down around the edges.

4 Cook for about 19-21 minutes. Carefully remove, cool & enjoy!

Cheese Breadsticks

Let's Get Ready!

- 1 piece of crescent roll dough about the size of your pan

- ½ tablespoon melted butter

- Pinch of garlic salt

- 2 tablespoons shredded cheese

- Marinara Sauce to dip in (optional)

Let's Cook!

1 Preheat oven according to manufacturers directions. Spray pan with nonstick spray.

2 Place dough on pan and flatten out to cover bottom of pan.

3 Combine melted butter and garlic salt. Brush on top of dough

4 Sprinkle cheese on top

5 Cook for approximately 10-12 minutes

6 Remove and cool. Cut into 3 separate sticks. Enjoy with marinara sauce (optional)

Chocolate Pancake

Let's Get Ready!

- 4 tablespoons "complete - just add water" pancake mix
- 1 ½ teaspoons sugar
- 1 ½ teaspoons unsweetened cocoa powder
- 3 tablespoons water

Let's Cook!

1. Preheat oven according to manufacturers directions. Spray molds with nonstick cooking spray

2. Combine pancake mix, cocoa, sugar. Mix well.

3. Add water and mix well.

4. Pour into pan and cook for about 9-10 minutes.

5. Top with your choice of toppings (Whipped topping, syrup, etc…)

Sprinkles Pancake

Let's Get Ready!

- 4 tablespoons "complete - just add water" pancake mix
- ½ tablespoon Sprinkles
- 3 tablespoons water

Let's Cook!

1. Preheat oven according to manufacturers directions. Spray molds with nonstick cooking spray

2. Combine pancake mix and water together and mix well. Pour into pan.

3. Sprinkle the sprinkles over the top of the uncooked pancake and gently glide over top with the back of a spoon to press into pancake batter.

4. Cook for approximately 9-10 minutes. Carefully remove and cool.

5. Top with your choice of toppings (Whipped topping, syrup, etc…)

FROSTING

Tips for **FABULOUS** Frosting

- You can substitute heavy whipping cream or half and half for milk. It gives it a GREAT taste.

- If your frosting is too thin, you can add more powdered sugar or let it set in the refrigerator for about 15 minutes.

- If your frosting is too thick, you can add more milk.

- Do **NOT** use hot chocolate mix in place of unsweetened cocoa. It will be way too sweet and will not have the great "chocolate" taste that you want.

Frosting Makes Life A Little Bit Sweeter

CHOCOLATE FROSTING

No Mixer Required!

Let's Make It!

Let's Get Ready!

- 6 tablespoons powdered sugar
- 2 tablespoons unsweetened cocoa powder
- Pinch of salt
- 4 tablespoons softened unsalted butter
- 1 teaspoon milk

1. Sift powdered sugar, unsweetened cocoa powder, and salt together into a bowl. Set aside.

2. In a separate small bowl, heat butter for about 10 seconds in microwave to get very soft, but NOT melted.

3. Form a hole in the middle of your powdered sugar mixture and drop butter into it. Add the teaspoon of milk.

4. Combine everything together by pressing together with a fork until you can use a spoon or small spatula. Mix very well.

Visit the Hasty Tasty Youtube channel!

Cream Cheese Frosting

No Mixer Required!

Let's Make It!

Let's Get Ready!

- 2 tablespoon softened Butter
- 2 tablespoon softened cream cheese
- ½ cup powdered sugar
- Pinch of salt
- Splash of Vanilla Extract

1. Heat butter and cream cheese in a microwave for about 10 seconds to get very soft, but do NOT melt. Set aside.

2. Mix together butter and cream cheese until smooth.

3. Add in Vanilla Extract.

4. Slowly sift in powdered sugar and pinch of salt. Mix together until smooth. It is normal to appear dry as you are mixing, but it will become more moistened as you mix it.

No Mixer Required!

Vanilla Buttercream

Let's Make It!

Let's Get Ready!

- 4 tablespoon softened unsalted butter
- 6 tablespoons powdered sugar
- Pinch of salt
- ¼ teaspoon Vanilla
- 1 teaspoon Milk

1. Heat butter in a microwave for about 10 seconds to get very soft, but don't melt. Set aside.

2. In a separate bowl, sift powdered sugar and pinch of salt together.

3. Form a hole in the middle of your powdered sugar mixture and drop butter into it. Add the vanilla and milk.

4. Combine everything together by pressing together with a fork until you can use a spoon or small spatula. Mix very well.

5. Optional: Add in a few drops of food coloring to change the color of your frosting! Mix well.

No Mixer Required!

PEANUT BUTTER

Let's Make It!

Let's Get Ready!

- 6 tablespoons powdered sugar
- Pinch salt
- 2 tablespoons softened unsalted butter
- 2 tablespoons peanut butter
- 1 teaspoon milk

1. Sift powdered sugar and pinch of salt into small bowl.

2. In a separate bowl, heat your butter in the microwave for about 10 seconds to get it very soft (not melted though!)

3. Add peanut butter to butter and mix together. I use a fork and press the ingredients down until I can mix with a spoon. It's normal to be stiff.

4. Form a hole in the middle of your powdered sugar mixture and drop peanut butter mixture into it. Add the teaspoon of milk.

5. Combine everything together by pressing together with a fork until you can use a spoon or small spatula. Mix very well.

Cutout & Laminate

Let them take their imagination to the next level with these fun bakery accessories! I <u>**HIGHLY recommend that you LAMINATE them**</u> for continued use. You can purchase the self laminating sheets online or from big box retailers to do it yourself, or most office supply stores can help you! This also allows your little chef to use **dry erase markers** and wipe off for re-use. They LOVE it!!

Front of Menu / Back of Menu   The front of your menu shows your customers what you have available. All they need to do is flip it over to the back to choose from the different flavors!

Order form   Use a dry erase marker to easily mark what your customer wants to order! Once you've served up their delicious food, just wipe off the order form and you're ready for the next customer.

Open Sign / Closed Sign   Make sure that everyone knows when you're OPEN or CLOSED with your bakery sign. Use a hole punch to punch two holes in the top and place a string or ribbon through it to easily hang wherever you want! Flip from side to side as you open & close.

Today's Special / Today's Special SOLD OUT   Let everyone know what the Special of the Day is by marking it on your sign. Punch two holes in it with a hole puncher and run a ribbon or string through to easily hang it anywhere. You can also prop it on a small easel on your "bakery" counter. Don't forget to use a dry erase marker so that you can change the Special tomorrow! Flip it over to let everyone know when you are sold out.

Order Here   Step right up and place your order! Make sure that your customers know where to go with your "Order Here" sign.

Name Tags

Sign to go on Tip Jar

Customer Credit Card This is one way your customer may pay you

Bill Give this to your customer so that they know how much they owe

Credit Card Receipt If they pay by credit card, give them this to sign their name

Play Cash & Coin

FLAVORS

Cakes & Cupcakes

Vanilla
Chocolate
Choc & Peanut Butter
Banana Split

Peanut Butter & Chocolate
Peanut Butter & Jelly
Red Velvet
Chocolate Covered Strawberry

Unicorn Cake
Cookies & Cream
Cake Mix Brownies

Cookies

Strawberries & Cream
Snickerdoodle

Lemonade
Chocolate Pudding

Chocolate Chip
Sprinkles

Pizza

English Muffin Pizza
Crescent Roll Pizza
Cheese Bread Sticks

Cinnamon Dessert Pizza
Strawberry Dessert Pizza
Chocolate & Peanut Butter Dessert Pizza

Just Too Good to Leave Out

Chocolate Pancakes

Sprinkles Pancakes

Hot Ham & Cheese

Frosting

Chocolate Buttercream
Vanilla Buttercream

Peanut Butter
Cream Cheese

Hasty Tasty Bakery

Please Come In

OPEN

HASTY TASTY
Bakery

May I Take Your Order Please?

 ☐

 ☐

 ☐

Other: ☐

 ☐

 ☐

 ☐

MILK $.75 ☐

Flavor: _____

Total $ _____

Today's Special

HASTY TASTY
Bakery

Hasty Tasty
CHEF

Order Here

Todays Special

Sold Out

HASTY TASTY
Bakery

Head Pastry Chef

Bakery Manager

TIPS
are
Appreciated

1234 5678 9123 4567

VALID THRU 12/25

Hasty Tasty Valued Customer

CREDIT CARD

Hasty Tasty Check

Thank You!
Please come again.

112066

Item	Price
Total	

(704) 444-1717

Merchant ID: 1111   Ref #: 106

Sale

xxxxxxxxxxxx1010
MC   Entry Method: SWIPE
CREDIT SALE

Subtotal: _____

Gratutity: _____

Total: _____

Signature:

_____

Merchant Copy

Thank You!
Please Come Again

 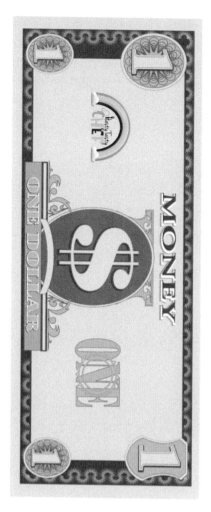 

Thank you so much for being a part of the Hasty Tasty Family! ♥

Made in the USA
Las Vegas, NV
30 October 2022

58411225R00029